C000256457

North East Life in the 1980s

by Andrew Clark & Sharyn Taylor

'A taste of things to come' – an advert announcing the opening of Carrefour on 29th April 1986. The French supermarket was the first major retailer to open at the MetroCentre. The store, later taken over by Gateway and then Asda, was demolished to make way for an extension to the Red Mall which was opened in 2004.

Copyright Andrew Clark & Sharyn Taylor 2018

First published in 2018 by

Summerhill Books
PO Box 1210, Newcastle-upon-Tyne NE99 4AH

www.summerhillbooks.co.uk

email: summerhillbooks@yahoo.co.uk

ISBN: 978-1-911385-20-2

No part of this publication may be reproduced, stored in a mechanical retrieval system, or transmitted, in any form or by any means, electronic, mechanical, photocopying, recording or otherwise, without prior permission of the authors.

Contents

NISSAN
BRITAIN'S
BLUEBIRD
BEHIND THE SCENES AND ON THE ROAD

NEWCASTLE CITY HALL
FOR 7 DAYS ONLY
BOOKING INFORMATION
FULL DETAILS OF ALL VENUES ON THE 45 SHOW
CHRISTMAS TOUR

The most dangerous choices are made with the heart.
MELANIE GRIFFITH
TOMMY LEE JONES
STING
SEAN BEAN
STORMY MONDAY
ATLANTIC ENTERTAINMENT GROUP
BRITISH SCREEN FILM FOUR INTERNATIONAL
MOVING PICTURE COMPANY
MELANIE GRIFFITH • TOMMY LEE JONES • STING • SEAN BEAN
"STORMY MONDAY" MIKE FIGGIS
ANDREW McALPINE SANDY POWELL
DAVID MARTIN ROGER DEAKINS
NIGEL STAFFORD-CLARK MIKE FIGGIS

TUNE INTO THE TUBE ON RECORD
MEGA HITS FROM — FRANKIE GOES TO HOLLYWOOD • THE JAM • U2 • EURYTHMICS • WHAM • PAUL YOUNG
ICICLE WORKS • THE ASSEMBLY • AZTEC CAMERA • THE CURE • YAZOO • DEPECHE MODE • AND MANY MORE

Keith Arkle with pony 'Tom', underground at Ellington Colliery in 1985.

Acknowledgements

The authors would like to thank the following who have kindly helped with this book:

Alan Brett, John Carlson, Harry & Pauline Clark, Philip Curtis, Peter Gibson, Jack Hair, Dorothy Hall, Paul Heslop, Tom Hutchinson, George Nairn, Francis Newman, Deborah Purnell, Charlie Steel, Mary Taylor, Natalie Taylor, Neil Taylor and John Yearnshire.

The Chronicle, The Journal, Northern Echo, Sunderland Echo
Gateshead Library, Newcastle Library, North Tyneside Libraries
Beamish Museum, West Newcastle Picture History Collection
Alamy

Bibliography

Annfield Plain & District by Jack Hair, The People's History

Around Gateshead by John Carlson & Joyce Carlson, The People's History

Ashington Coal Company – The Five Collieries by Mike Kirkup, The People's History

Chester-le-Street The Twentieth Century by George Nairn & Dorothy Hall, The People's History

Ellington Colliery Through The Years by Neil Taylor, Summerhill Books

Gateshead Remembered by Anthea Lang, Summerhill Books

Monkseaton Village Volume Two by Charlie Steel, Summerhill Books

Penshaw & Shiney Row – Then and Now by Lena Cooper, Summerhill Books

Southwick by Peter Gibson, The People's History

Tynemouth Remembered by Charlie Steel, Summerhill Books

Woodhorn by Mike Kirkup, Woodhorn Press

Introduction

This book is a follow up to our previous publication *North East Life in the 1970s*. Like that edition, we are not telling the complete story of the decade but highlighting some of the major events of that time. We, the authors, were both teenagers during the 1980s and we share our memories of fashions; early computers and video recorders; popular toys and games; happy times at Metroland; first holidays abroad and concerts at Newcastle City Hall.

The 1980s saw many new developments in the region such as the opening of the Metro transport system, the MetroCentre and Nissan's car factory. The end of the decade also saw plans unveiled that would be the start of the regeneration of the Quayside at Newcastle and Gateshead.

The region's industrial heritage of shipbuilding and mining is also recalled. In 1983 miners and their families celebrated the centenary of the Durham Miners' Gala only for the following year to see the start of a bitter industrial dispute. Later in the decade shipbuilding came to an end in Sunderland with thousands of job losses in what was once a thriving industry.

We feature subjects such as the music of the 1980s as well as television shows and films set in the North East. The hugely popular TV series *Auf Wiedersehen, Pet* made household names of Geordie actors Tim Healy, Kevin Whately and Jimmy Nail.

There were also many other days to remember such as the *Tuxedo Princess* floating nightclub coming to the Tyne and the biggest musicians in the world playing at St James' Park, Roker Park and Gateshead Stadium.

If any readers would like to share their memories (or spot themselves in photographs) we would be happy to hear from you. Please email us at: summerhillbooks@yahoo.co.uk

Below are some of our highlights from the 1980s.

Andrew Clark & Sharyn Taylor

Andrew's Favourites TV programmes

Auf Wiedersehen, Pet, Boys from the Blackstuff, Edge of Darkness

Favourite Films

Blade Runner, Blue Velvet, Raging Bull

First Concert

Haircut 100, Newcastle City Hall, 1982

First Holiday Abroad

Costa Brava, 1980

First Job

Habitat

Sharyn's Favourite TV programmes

Hart to Hart, Twin Peaks, The Wonder Years

Favourite Films

Annie, Flashdance, Ghostbusters

First Concert

Kylie Minogue, Mayfair, Newcastle, 1989

First Holiday Abroad

Salou, 1986

First Job

Mullers Bakers

Snapshots of the 1980s

In February 1984 it was announced that Nissan would build its first European car plant at Sunderland. An initial £50 million investment by the Japanese car maker, transformed the land around Sunderland Airfield into a high-tech car factory within two years.

Right: Work starts on the building of Nissan's factory with construction vehicles taking part in a ground-breaking ceremony.

The first Nissan Bluebird rolled off the production line in 1986. One of the first cars was later donated to Sunderland Museum & Winter Gardens to be displayed in an exhibition of the area's history. The workforce at this time was around 500 who produced 5,000 cars in the first year of production.

Left: The cover of a Nissan brochure for 'Britain's Bluebird' from 1986. In the background is the factory that built it. Thirty years later the Nissan plant employs around 7,000 workers and over nine million cars have been built since it first opened. One of their latest models is the Leaf – an electric, fuel efficient vehicle.

Right: 'We've Got Kevin!' – The programme for Kevin Keegan's first game for Newcastle United on 28th August 1982. The Magpies' manager, Arthur Cox, stunned the football world when he persuaded the star to come to Newcastle. The striker was one of the biggest names in football who, after winning every honour at Liverpool in the 1970s, was signed for a record-breaking fee by Hamburg. In Germany, Keegan was twice voted European Footballer of the Year. In 1980 he returned to England to play for Southampton and two years later signed for Newcastle. On his debut against QPR, Keegan scored the only goal in a 1-0 victory and ran to the fans at the Gallowgate End to celebrate. Promotion was clinched to the First Division at the end of the 1983-84 season and Keegan retired from playing football. His farewell to the fans was a friendly against Liverpool; leaving St James' Park in a helicopter.

Right: Runners taking part in the first Great North Run on Sunday 28th June 1981.

The race from Newcastle to South Shields was the idea of Brendan Foster who had started organising fun runs in the North East in the 1970s. For the first Great North Run 12,264 people started the race with 10,665 finishing. Around £1 million was raised for charity.

One of the runners taking part that day was footballer Kevin Keegan. At that time he was playing for Southampton and in a diplomatic gesture for the North East crowd ran in a shirt that was half black and white stripes and half red and white – to represent both Newcastle and Sunderland. Keegan promised to pay to charity 50 pence for every man who finished ahead of him and £1 for every woman. He finished the run in 490th place and paid out £250 to the Charlie Bear Charity raising money for cancer.

The winner of the 1981 race was Mike McLeod of Elswick Harriers in a time of 1 hour 3 minutes. Finishing second was Norwegian Oyvind Dahl and third was South Shields athlete Mike Kearns. Brendan Foster finished in 20th place. The winner of the men's wheelchair race was Alan Robinson. Twenty-year-old Karen Goldhawk from South Shields was the first women to finish. After the race she said: 'I'm pleased, although I'm tired. I was trying to be the first woman and when I was passing the men I thought "Why not?" I knew about Kevin Keegan giving the money to charity and I was thinking about it.'

The runners stream across the Tyne Bridge in 1981. Below them is the Quayside Market.

Mike McLeod – the winner of the first two Great North Runs. The Northumberland-born athlete went on to win the silver medal in the 10,000 metres at the 1984 Olympics in Los Angeles.

It is estimated that up to half a million people lined the route to cheer on the runners and provide the encouragement to complete the race in 1981. From these early beginnings the Great North Run is now one of the biggest running events in the world with over 50,000 people taking part each year. The winner of the four races since 2014 has been Sir Mo Farah.

My Great North Run

I've finished four Great North Runs and the highlight of the race for me, apart from the finish, is always near the start when you run across the Tyne Bridge. It's an amazing feeling to be among thousands of other runners with the crowds lining that iconic bridge cheering you on every step. However, once you are over the bridge it's a long way to the finishing line at South Shields.

Andrew Clark

Left: Herrington Colliery, near Penshaw. The colliery closed in 1985 and was one of a number that ceased working in the 1980s. Others included:

County Durham

Bearpark (closed 1984)
Blackhall (1981)
Boldon (1982)
East Hetton (1983)
Eden (1980)
Eppleton (1986)
Herrington (1985)
Horden (1987)
Houghton (1981)
Marley Hill (1983)
Sacriston (1985)
Seaham (1988)
South Hetton (1982)
South Medomsley (1980)

Northumberland

Ashington (1988)
Backworth (1980)
Bates, Blyth (1986)
Brenkley, Seaton Burn (1985)
Whittle, Alnwick (1987)
Woodhorn (1981)

Left: Herrington Colliery during demolition with Penshaw Monument in the background. The former mining site was landscaped into a popular country park.

Woodhorn Colliery had been operating for almost a century when it closed in 1981. Unlike other former North East pits, Woodhorn was to have a new lease of life when it was converted into a colliery museum which opened in 1989.

In the early part of this century Woodhorn Museum was expanded. A new building was opened in 2006 that includes the Northumberland County Archives. The museum is also home to a collection of art by the Ashington Group – 'The Pitmen Painters'.

In 1980 the Federation Brewery moved to Dunston near to where the MetroCentre was later built. This new modern plant replaced the Fed's old premises behind the Central Station in Newcastle that was its home for fifty years. The brewery had been established in 1919 when social and workingmen's clubs came together to form The Northern Clubs Federation to supply beer to their premises. The 1980s were hard times for the North East clubs with many closing over the following decades and the brewery itself was closed in 2010. To the right of the Fed is the Lancastrian Suite which today is still one of the most popular conference and banqueting centres in the North East.

The launch of the *Colima* from Laing's shipyard on the Wear on 30th July 1984. A hundred men worked through their holidays so the ship would be ready for a high tide. There was to be only one more ship launch from Laing's before the yard was closed.

The Digital Decade

Right: Pupils from Cambo First School near Morpeth using their BBC Micro computer in 1983. The Acorn Computer Company designed and built the BBC Micro as part of the corporation's computer literacy project. The computer was launched in 1981 and over a million were sold with many schools acquiring them.

In 1982 the BBC broadcast *The Computer Programme* where Chris Serle – best known for the show *That's Life!* –was shown the basics of computer programming using the BBC Micro.

Memories of a Sinclair User

My first experience of computers was at school where a whole class had to share the three BBC Micros we had. Every week in our computer studies class we would learn some basic programming and I remember spending weeks on a project to work out our gas bills from home. Also in the class we would watch videos of the BBC's *The Computer Programme.* My parents bought me a second hand Sinclair ZX81 (*right*) which I thought was great at the time. It had a tiny memory of only 1k but you could get an external memory pack that connected into the back of the computer that increased this to 16k. I found the memory pack very flimsy and the slightest movement would break the connection and crash the computer. Programmes on cassettes could also be loaded on to the ZX81 using a 'shoebox' type tape recorder (*seen in the photograph above next to the BBC Micro*). Some of the games I remember were 3D Monster Maze, Chess and Frogger. Magazines such as *Sinclair User* would also feature programmes for games. I would spend hours typing in the code but the slightest mistake and it wouldn't work – so I had to start all over again.

Andrew Clark

Sinclair ZX Spectrum

16K or 48K RAM... full-size moving-key keyboard... colour and sound... high-resolution graphics...

From only £125!

An advert for the Sinclair ZX Spectrum – the successor to the ZX81. The Spectrum had an improved keyboard, colour, sound and high-resolution graphics. The price for a 16k model was £125 with the 48k model being £155.

The *Sinclair User* magazine from December 1984 had a 100 Ghostbusters games to be won.

1980s Digital Time Line

1980
May 22nd – The arcade game Pac-Man is released in Japan and worldwide later in the year.

1981
March 5th – The ZX81 is launched by Clive Sinclair with over 1.5 million sold worldwide.

July 9th – Donkey Kong is released by Nintendo.

December 1st – The BBC Micro is launched by Acorn Computer Company.

1982
January 7th – The Commodore 64 home computer is launched.

January 30th – The first computer virus, the Elk Cloner, infects Apple II computers via floppy disks.

December – Adobe Systems is founded. In later years they produce software including Photoshop, PageMaker, InDesign, FreeHand, Acrobat and Dreamweaver.

December – AutoCAD – the Computer Aided Design programme is launched.

1983
March 9th – The 3D printer is invented by Chuck Hull.

1984
January 24th – Apple starts selling the Macintosh personal computer.

June 6th – Tetris, the puzzle video game, is released in the Soviet Union.

Pupils at Denton Road School, Newcastle, with their BBC Micro in 1983. On the screen are the words: 'Type your name on the dotted line.'

Workers at Swan Hunter's shipyard using Computer Aided Design (CAD).

1985
January 10th – The Sinclair C5 (*right*) is launched. It is a battery-assisted three-wheeled vehicle by Clive Sinclair, costing £399.

July 24th – The country domain '.uk' is registered.

August 13th – The Sinclair C5 ceases production after producing around 12,000 vehicles with many unsold.

November 20th – Microsoft Corporation releases the first version of Windows – Windows 1.0.

1986
January 19th – The first PC virus, Brain, starts to spread.

April 7th – Clive Sinclair sells the rights to ZX Spectrum and other designs to Alan Sugar's Amstrad company for £5 million.

1989
July 31st – Nintendo releases the Game Boy portable video game system.

Left: A late 1980s Amstrad computer. The word Amstrad comes from shortening **A**lan **M**ichael **S**ugar **Trad**ing.

Metro Memories

Left: The cover of the booklet 'Meet Your Metro', published in 1977 by Tyne & Wear Transport to inform passengers of the new system. The first plans for the Metro came from a local report in the early 1970s to improve the transport links in Tyne and Wear. Work started in 1974 and six years later, on 11th August 1980, the Metro was opened with the first phase being between the Haymarket in Newcastle and Tynemouth – a total of fourteen stations. In May 1981 the second stage was opened from South Gosforth to Bank Foot.

Metro Facts

When the Metro was first planned it was known simply as 'the rapid transport system' so in 1972 a competition was held to pick a name for the project. The winning entry was 'Tran-Cit', however this name was never used. Two years later the Passenger Transport Executive announced that the new system would be called 'The Metro'.

The first fares were an equivalent cost to bus services. The longest journey, Haymarket to Tynemouth, was 38 pence. For a trip from the Haymarket to Jesmond the fare was 8 pence.

Thousands of homes near the Metro's first route received information packs to give advice on the new system. Open days were also held at all of the fourteen stations that were operational in the first section. People were informed of the new ticket machines and barriers.

The Metro was the first railway in the UK to operate using the metric system with distances measured by the kilometre.

Smoking has never been allowed on the Metro and it was one of the first complete bans on a transport system in the UK. In 1980 the penalty for smoking was £50.

The Queen Elizabeth II Metro Bridge (*right*) was opened in November 1981 by the Queen. Built for a cost of £4.9 million, the new bridge allowed the Metro to cross the Tyne and opened up the route to Heworth via Gateshead. In 1984 the line was extended to South Shields via Hebburn and Jarrow.

Another Metro bridge was opened in 1982 – the Byker Viaduct that carries the St James' to Tynemouth section of the line.

Right: The train to Heworth at Gateshead Station.

The Metro's cost up to 1980 was £280 million with 70 percent coming from the Government and the remaining money from Tyne and Wear Council. In its first full year of service, 1984-85, there were over 60 million passenger journeys.

The first Metro line in 1980 used part of an old railway network that ran through Newcastle and North Tyneside. Some routes had been open since the 1830s and in 1904 the lines started to be electrified. This was known as the North Tyneside Loop and ran through Wallsend, North Shields, Whitley Bay, Benton and South Gosforth. In the 1960s British Rail changed the rolling stock to diesel which were slower than the electric trains they were replacing.

The Metro taking over the North Tyneside Loop meant that some of the historic stations on the line were used. They were all closed for a short time and re-opened after being converted to serve Metro passengers.

These included Whitley Bay Station (*above left*) which was used for decades by the thousands of visitors to the seaside resort. Another station is West Monkseaton which has an Art Deco exterior (*left*). The station was first opened in 1933.

Tynemouth Station (*seen on the left in the early 1900s*) was opened in 1882. As can be seen in this postcard the station has a large interior with ornate decorative features and glass roof. In 1987 a group called the Friends of Tynemouth Station was formed to help protect and promote the building that has Grade II listing status. In the 21st century a major renovation took place to bring it back to its former glory. A popular weekend market has been running at the station for many years.

The Miners' Strike

Right: Arthur Scargill with Labour Leader Michael Foot at the Bedlington Miners' Picnic. In 1982 Arthur Scargill became leader of the National Union of Mineworkers, succeeding Joe Gormley who had led the miners during the strikes of the 1970s.

A year after Scargill's appointment Ian MacGregor became chairman of the National Coal Board. He had previously been at British Steel which had seen redundancies and plant closures under his management. Prime Minister Margaret Thatcher had personally approved MacGregor's move to the NCB and his brief was to close pits.

Mike Kirkup, former miner and author of *Ashington – The Biggest Mining Village in the World*, said: 'The then Tory leader, Margaret Thatcher pursued a head-on confrontation with miners' leader Arthur Scargill – an irresistible force against an immovable object. As the song says *Something's Gotta Give*. A bitter strike began.'

In March 1984, following an announcement that 20 pits were to close, miners throughout the country started industrial action. However, not all men went on strike with many miners in the collieries in the Midlands and some in the North East continuing to work. This led to confrontation outside of pits with striking miners trying to stop workers crossing picket lines and clashes with the police were common.

Left: Striking miners attempt to stop buses carrying workers entering Ellington Colliery and are held back by the police.

In September 1984 talks were held in Edinburgh between Ian MacGregor, and Arthur Scargill but no agreement could be reached to end the strike. The following month, the High Court ruled that the miners' strike was unlawful as no national ballot had been held before it had began. The NUM was fined £200,000 with Arthur Scargill having to pay £1,000 for contempt of court.

Left: Four men on the picket line at Lynemouth. At its peak the strike involved over 140,000 workers.

As the strike dragged on it became increasingly difficult for miners and their families to make ends meet. Kitchens were set up to feed people, such as the one on the right in Ashington. Hardship money was paid out of union funds but it only covered the basics. Miners struggled to pay their mortgages and keep cars on the road while most luxuries had to stop. The long strike also put a strain on marriages.

After almost a year, the strike ended on 3rd March 1985.

Right: A number of support groups were set up and here are the women of Ellington who backed the miners of their community.

Below: Two photographs showing the miners on a march through Ashington after the end of the strike. Banners were held high and the men were joined by their families and friends.

After the strike a number of collieries in the region were closed. One of the pits, Seaham Colliery, ended production in 1988 and is seen on the right awaiting demolition. The following decade saw mining come to an end at Dawdon, Easington, Murton, Vane Tempest, Wearmouth and Westoe. Ellington Colliery, the last deep coal mine in the North East, was closed in 2005.

Sounds of the 1980s

Above: Lindisfarne performing at one of their Christmas concerts at a packed Newcastle City Hall in 1980. Thousands of fans were entertained with the group's classic hits – *Fog on the Tyne, Run for Home, Lady Eleanor* and *Meet Me on the Corner*.

Left: A brochure advertising Lindisfarne's Christmas shows in 1986. As well as seven nights in Newcastle, the Geordie group also went on a nationwide tour with 45 concerts in total. The brochure advised North East fans:

'You can be certain that all the City Hall shows will be complete sell-outs. Be sure of getting your tickets for Lindisfarne's legendary City Hall shows by booking now!'

Right: In 1984 Lindisfarne were special guests when Bob Dylan appeared at St James' Park. Also on the bill was Santana. Before the concert, Ray Laidlaw of Lindisfarne said:

'What makes this gig special is that it's at St James' Park. We've always played different sized places. Big festivals like this, concert halls and smaller places. The night before we play with Dylan we're doing a benefit for the miners at a hall in Newbiggin. It only holds three hundred people but they'll get exactly the same show.'

Mark Knopfler (*right*) was born in Glasgow and spent his early years growing up in Blyth. With his younger brother, David (rhythm guitar), he founded the band Dire Straits in 1977. Other early members were John Illsley (bass), Pick Withers (drums) and Alan Clark (keyboards) from Great Lumley. Their first hit single was *Sultans of Swing* in 1978 reaching the top ten in the UK and US charts. The record showcased Mark Knopfler's distinct lead guitar sound. Further chart success was achieved with their singles *Romeo and Juliet* and *Private Investigations*.

In the early 1980s Knopfler became interested in writing music for films. His management approached film makers and the producer David Puttnam asked him to write the music for *Local Hero*. The 1983 film, starring Burt Lancaster, is the story of an oil company wanting to drill off the Scottish coast. The soundtrack was nominated for a British Academy Award and the tune *Going Home: Theme of the Local Hero* is played before Newcastle's home games.

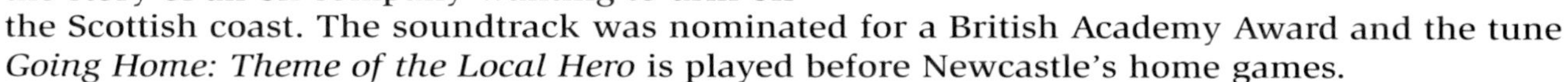

On 13th May 1985 Dire Straits released their fifth studio album *Brothers in Arms* (*left*) which was a massive worldwide hit. It won two Grammies in 1986 and it was the first compact disc to sell over a million. The album went on to sell over 30 million copies. The first single released was *Money for Nothing,* which included vocals from Sting. Other singles were *Walk of Life* and the title track *Brothers In Arms*.

After the band's 1985-86 world tour of over 200 shows, Knopfler continued on his solo career and wrote the soundtrack to the film *The Princess Bride* in 1987. Dire Straits then regrouped for the Nelson Mandella 70th Birthday Tribute Concert at Wembley in 1988. The band released their final album *On Every Street* in 1991.

Dave Stewart (*right with Annie Lennox*) was born in Sunderland in 1952 and in his teens he formed the folk rock band Longdancer. Although signed to Elton John's record label, this first band did not achieve success. In the 1970s he was living in London and met Annie Lennox. With Peet Coombes, also from Sunderland, they formed the group The Catch and then later The Tourists. Their biggest hit was *I Only Want To Be With You*, a cover of a Dusty Springfield song, that reached number four in the charts in 1979. After The Tourist split up, Stewart and Lennox became the Eurythmics in 1980. Success followed three years later with the release of their second album *Sweet Dreams (Are Made Of This)* with the title track reaching number two in the single charts. It was kept off the top spot by The Police's *Every Breath You Take*. Other best selling singles included: *Love Is A Stranger, Whose That Girl?, There Must Be An Angel (Playing With My Heart)* and *Sisters Are Doin' It For Themselves* with Aretha Franklin. The Eurythmics split in 1990 and Stewart worked on a number of other projects including forming the band The Spiritual Cowboys as well as recording songs with Paul McCartney and Bono and Edge of U2. The Eurythmics reformed in 1999 before splitting again in 2005.

In 1982 Tyne Tees Television launched the music programme *The Tube* on Channel 4. The show, presented by Paula Yates and Jools Holland (*right*), was first broadcast on Bonfire Night. Over the next five years the biggest names in the music world came to perform at the Tyne Tees Studios on City Road in Newcastle. The name of the programme came from a plastic, tubular walkway that linked one of the studios to the street.

Some of the acts who appeared on *The Tube* include: The Jam, Tina Turner, Madonna, Robert Plant, U2, ZZ Top, Frankie Goes to Hollywood, Duran Duran, The Eurythmics, The Cure and The Smiths. The programme also featured a number of North East personalties such as the Newcastle photographer Jimmy Forsyth, comedian Vic Reeves and Sunderland punk band The Toy Dolls who played the first song on the show.

In 1983 a five hour special was broadcast called *A Midsummer Night's Tube* which included a documentary on Duran Duran filmed in France.

In 1984 a compilation album of some of the bands who appeared on the show was released. *The Tube's* neon sign logo was used on the cover.

Left: Duran Duran on the front cover of the *TV Times* in June 1983 for *A Midsummer Night's Tube.* Band member Andy Taylor from Cullercoats is on the far right.

The Tube was a good supporter of the local music scene and featured a number of groups from independent record label Kitchenware Records. The label, formed in Newcastle in 1982 by Keith Armstrong, Paul Ludford and Phil Mitchell, signed North East bands Prefab Sprout, The Kane Gang (*right*), Hurrah! and Martin Stephenson and the Dainties.

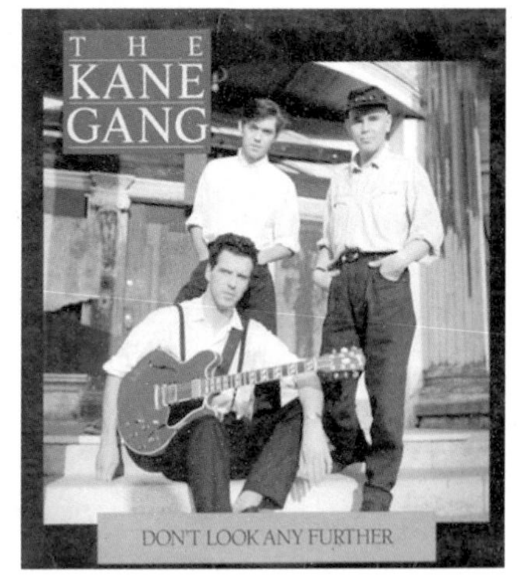

The Kang Gang's biggest hit was the single *Closest Thing to Heaven* which reached number 12 in the UK charts and saw them appear on *Top of the Pops*. Their lead vocalist Martin Brammer from Seaham has gone on to write songs for the Lighthouse Family, Tina Turner, Olly Murs, Beverley Knight, Mark Owen, James Morrison and Sheena Easton.

Prefab Sprout's most successful album was *From Langley Park to Memphis* (*left*) whose title was inspired by their County Durham roots. It reached number five in the album charts and includes two of the band's best known singles – *The King of Rock 'n' Roll* and *Cars and Girls*. Prefab Sprout was founded by the singer Paddy McAloon who has also wrote songs for Kylie Minogue, Cher and Jimmy Nail.

The Pet Shop Boys – Neil Tennant and Chris Lowe – on the front cover of the magazine *Smash Hits* from February 1986. Neil Tennant was born in North Shields and grew up in Newcastle after his family moved there when he was young. He spent the late 1970s and early '80s working in publishing and became the assistant editor of *Smash Hits* in 1983. At this time Tennant was writing songs with Chris Lowe and success was to come in the mid 1980s with singles such as *West End Girls*, *Opportunities (Let's Make Lots of Money)*, *It's a Sin*, *Rent* and, with Dusty Springfield, *What Have I Done To Deserve This*.

Chris Rea (*right*) had his greatest success in the 1980s with three platinum-selling albums – *On The Beach*, *Dancing With Strangers* and *The Road to Hell*. The title track of *The Road to Hell* gave him his best selling single in the UK and his first top ten chart hit. Other popular singles for the Middlesbrough-born singer-songwriter in the 1980s were *Let's Dance* and *Driving Home for Christmas*.

The most popular singles of the 1980s

1980 – Don't Stand So Close to Me
by The Police

1981 – Tainted Love
by Soft Cell

1982 – Come On Eileen
by Dexys Midnight Runners

1983 – Karma Chameleon
by Culture Club

1984 – Do They Know It's Christmas?
by Band Aid

1985 – The Power of Love
by Jennifer Rush

1986 – Don't Leave Me This Way
by The Communards

1987 – Never Gonna Give You Up
by Rick Astley

1988 – Mistletoe and Wine
by Cliff Richard

1989 – Ride on Time
by Black Box

The most popular albums

1980 – Super Trouper
by ABBA

1981 – Kings of the Wild Frontier
by Adam and the Ants

1982 – Love Songs
by Barbra Streisand

1983 – Thriller
by Michael Jackson

1984 – Can't Slow Down
by Lionel Richie

1985 – Brothers in Arms
by Dire Straits

1986 – True Blue
by Madonna

1987 – Bad
by Michael Jackson

1988 – Kylie
by Kylie Minogue

1989 – Ten Good Reasons
by Jason Donovan

Shipyard Stories

Right: The Queen Mother talks to people at Swan Hunter's Wallsend shipyard on the day she launched the aircraft carrier HMS *Ark Royal* in 1981.

Memories of Swan Hunter's are recalled by one worker at the yard in the early 1980s:

'We were working on the aircraft carrier *Illustrious* when the Falklands War started. It was nearing completion and we had to speed up so it would be ready to go to the South Atlantic. I think we were working seven days a week and twelve hour shifts so they were long, long days. I had a lump in my throat the day we finished working on the ship because it was like losing a part of you. We had become very attached to the ship and we were very proud of it. It almost became like a home to us as we spent so long on board.

'Then we built her sister ship the *Ark Royal* which was another one that I worked on from the beginning to the end. Because of the *Ark Royal's* status, and the history that famous name has, I had an even bigger lump in my throat when that one went away. It was a ship where everybody seemed to muck in together no matter what problems we had. A lot of men were really proud to be part of that ship.

'As the ships were being finished off you could take your family on board to have a look around. I took my dad to see the *Ark Royal*. He had worked in the yards for over 30 years – mostly as a driller – but had been out of the yards for a few years through ill health. When I took him on to the *Ark Royal* I had placed a drilling machine at the top of the gangway and when he saw it he had tears in his eyes. His memories came flooding back when we went round the ship. He really missed working in the yards.'

Left: The launch of HMS *York* from Swan Hunter's in June 1982. Note how close the workers and their families are as the ship enters the water. HMS *York* was in service for 30 years and supported HMS *Ark Royal* during the invasion of Iraq in 2003.

Right: The launch of the *Mitla* on 3rd May 1985. It was to be last ship built at Laing's shipyard on the Wear.

Former Sunderland headmaster Philip Curtis recalls the launch of the *Mitla*:

'In 1985, as part of the local studies curriculum, I took a class from Redby Junior School to Laing's to watch the launch of the *Mitla*. We all went with great anticipation of a memorable spectacle and weren't disappointed. To see, close up, a brand new ship seemingly perfectly balanced on its wooden chocks certainly took the breath away. I remember the arrival of the launch party and the extravagant fur coats and expensive jewellery adorning the wives of the shipowners. As the final chock was hammered away and the champagne duly delivered, the accompanying cheers of the workers and spectators were quickly drowned out by the roar of the drag chains. Balloons and coloured smoke were released from the ship as it slid gracefully into the water. I asked the worker who had hammered away the final white painted chock if I could take it as a souvenir. I carried it back to school where it was proudly displayed alongside the children's accounts of the day. At the end of term I took home this precious piece of Sunderland shipbuilding history wondering what to do with it. My wife, Margaret, solved the problem. She stuck it in the shed and waited until I had forgotten all about it before discretely disposing of it during a spring clean. Another piece of Sunderland's heritage lost forever!'

Left: The final ships built in Sunderland – a fleet of ferries – moored by Wearmouth Bridge in the late 1980s.

The shipyards on the River Wear were closed in December 1988 and thousands of workers lost their jobs. A £45 million pound package of Government and European money was given to Sunderland to redevelop the former shipbuilding sites at Southwick and North Sands. As part of that deal shipbuilding had to cease in Sunderland for five years, later increased to ten.

Left: The North Sands site, seen here in its final days, was later redeveloped into the National Glass Centre and a campus for Sunderland University. The shipbuilding complex at Southwick was demolished in 1991 and now a business and retail park occupies the land. The Pallion shipyard – the biggest indoor yard in the world when it was opened in 1975 – was acquired by an engineering firm in 1991.

TV Times

One of the most popular television shows of the 1980s was *Auf Wiedersehen, Pet*, the story of seven British workers, including three Geordie brickies, and their exploits on a German building site. The series was created by Franc Roddam, a film director and television producer, from an idea of Mick Connell a Stockton bricklayer. Norton-born Roddam also created the cookery show *Masterchef*.

Auf Wiedersehen, Pet starred three North East actors – Tim Healy, Kevin Whately and Jimmy Nail – alongside Timothy Spall, Gary Holton, Pat Roach and Christopher Fairbank. The series was filmed on location in Dusseldorf and at Elstree Studios where the German building site was recreated. It was produced by Central Television and first broadcast on ITV between November 1983 and February 1984.

The success of the first series led to a follow up shown in 1986. This time the 'magnificent seven' were seen working in the Midlands and then Spain. Other North East actors who featured in the series included: Julia Tobin (Neville's wife), Val McLane (Dennis' sister), Melanie Hill (Barry's girlfriend) and Su Elliot (Oz's wife).

Sadly Gary Holton died before filming of the second series was completed. Scripts had to be rewritten and a double was used for some of his character's scenes.

The cast of *Auf Wiedersehen, Pet* – Tim Healy (Dennis Patterson), Kevin Whately (Neville Hope), Jimmy Nail (Oz Osborne), Timothy Spall (Barry Taylor, a Brummie), Gary Holton (Wayne Norris, a Cockney), Pat Roach (Bomber Busbridge from the West Country) and Christopher Fairbank (Moxey, a Scouser).

Left: Dick Clement and Ian La Frenais – the writers of *Auf Wiedersehen, Pet*. Monkseaton-born Ian La Frenais started his creative partnership with Dick Clement from Essex in the 1960s. Their earliest success was the North East comedy *The Likely Lads*. They also wrote the prison sitcom *Porridge* starring Ronnie Barker. Moving to California in the late 1970s, the writers worked on film scripts including the James Bond film *Never Say Never Again*. La Frenais returned to his North East roots with the hit series *Auf Wiedersehen, Pet*. He later worked on *Lovejoy* with Ian McShane as the loveable antiques dealer. In the early 1990s, he re-united with Jimmy Nail for the Tyneside detective series *Spender*.

For the three North East actors, *Auf Wiedersehen, Pet* was the start of very successful television careers. Tim Healy went on to appear in several other shows including *Waterloo Road*, *Benidorm* and *Still Open All Hours*. Kevin Whately is perhaps best know for being the sidekick of Inspector Morse and having his own series based on the character – *Lewis*.

Jimmy Nail had hit records with *Love Don't Live Here Any More* and *Ain't No Doubt* as well as creating and starring in *Spender* and *Crocodile Shoes*. He has also appeared in the films *Evita*, *Danny the Champion of the World* and *Still Crazy*.

In 2002 *Auf Wiedersehen, Pet* returned for a new series with a plot based around the Teesside Transporter Bridge being relocated to America. The BBC show brought back six of the original cast with Noel Clarke playing the son of the Wayne Norris character.

Right: Actor Dennis Waterman poses for a photograph at Woodhorn Colliery while filming *The World Cup: A Captain's Tale.* Produced by Tyne Tees Television, the film told the story of the County Durham football team West Auckland who were England's entry for the Sir Thomas Lipton Trophy in 1909 and 1911. The trophy was one of the first international football cup competitions in the world when it was played in Turin with teams from Italy, Germany and Switzerland taking part. West Auckland lifted the 1909 trophy by beating Swiss side FC Winterthur in the final. They returned two years later and again the won the competition by beating Juventus 6-1.

Seventy years later the film version of West Auckland's great victory starred Dennis Waterman as their captain. The actor, best known for *Minder,* was joined by Tim Healy and Richard Griffiths from the North East.

The West Auckland team with the Sir Thomas Lipton Trophy they won in 1909 and 1911.

Left: Extras in period costume at Woodhorn Colliery during filming of *The World Cup: A Captain's Tale.* The film was broadcast in June 1982, at the time of the World Cup in Spain, won by Italy.

Popular TV shows of the 1980s

Comedies: Blackadder, Dear John, Hi-de-Hi, Just Good Friends, Only Fools and Horses, Yes Minister and The Young Ones.

Dramas: Boys from the Blackstuff, Brideshead Revisited, Edge of Darkness, The Jewel in the Crown and The Singing Detective.

American shows: The A-Team, Cheers, Dallas, Dynasty, Hill Street Blues, Knight Rider, Miami Vice and Moonlighting.

Children's shows: The Adventure Game, Button Moon, Dramarama, Jonny Briggs, Postman Pat and Thomas the Tank Engine & Friends.

Quizzes and game shows: Blockbusters, Bob's Full House, Bullseye, Catchphrase, Play Your Cards Right and The Price is Right.

Supergran

The much loved *Supergran* with Gudrun Ure (*right*) in the title role as the grandmother with superpowers was first shown in 1985. Her archenemy, Scunner Campbell, was played by Iain Cuthbertson. The series, produced by Tyne Tees Television, was filmed in a number of locations around the North East including: Tynemouth, Whitley Bay, South Shields and Beamish. Many famous personalties and actors appeared in the show – George Best, Spike Milligan, Geoff Capes, Charles Hawtrey, Roy Kinnear and Patrick Troughton. The memorable theme tune was sung by Billy Connolly. Supergran was broadcast in over 60 countries worldwide and was a big hit in China.

Music, Drama & Quizzes from Tyne Tees

Tyne Tees Television, based on City Road in Newcastle, produced numerous programmes in the 1980s, including:

Razzmatazz – A junior version of *The Tube* that ran from June 1981 till January 1987. There was also an annual based on this very popular show (*left*).

The Roxy – ITV's rival to *Top of the Pops*, shown 1987-88.

Barriers – A drama starring Benedict Taylor searching for his adoptive parents, shown 1981-82.

Andy Robson – A children's drama set in Edwardian Northumberland, shown 1982-83.

Crosswits – A quiz show hosted by Barry Cryer and Tom O'Connor that was shown for thirteen years from 1985.

Byker Grove

In 1989 the BBC launched the children's TV series *Byker Grove* set in a Tyneside youth club. Much of the filming for the series was done at The Mitre (*right*) in the West End of Newcastle.

Some of those who got their first acting break in the show included: Ant McPartlin, Declan Donnelly, Jill Halfpenny, Donna Air and Charlie Hunnam who has found fame in Hollywood blockbusters such as *King Arthur: Legend of the Sword* and *Pacific Rim*.

There will be further memories of *Byker Grove* in the next book in this series – *North East Life in the 1990s*.

My Fifteen Minutes of Fame

When I left school I approached an agent for acting work who got me an audition for *Byker Grove*. My Dad gave me a lift to The Mitre in Newcastle and I met with the director and producer. I was put in front of a camera and asked to read the script. The part was for a girl called Mel who was a fan of a pop group. At the end of my audition I was told by the casting director that they would get back to me and a week later the phone rang and I had the part. I was so excited that soon I was going to appear on television. My agent gave me the script and I spent ages learning my lines. Next I had to go back to The Mitre for a rehearsal and a read through of the script with another girl who was also playing a fan of the group. I had three days of filming around Newcastle and I appeared in several scenes that in total lasted about quarter of an hour. Andy Warhol once said everyone would be famous for fifteen minutes – and that was my fifteen minutes of *Byker Grove* fame.

Sharyn Taylor

1980s TV Time Line

1980
March 21st – J.R. Ewing, played by Larry Hagman, is shot at the end of the third series of *Dallas*. Viewers have to wait until November to find out 'Who shot J.R.?'

1981
July 29th – A worldwide audience of over 700 million watch the broadcast of the wedding of the Prince of Wales and Lady Diana Spencer.

August 1st – MTV, the first 24-hour music channel, is launched. The first video to be shown is *Video Killed the Radio Star* by The Buggles. Trevor Horn of the band was born in Durham.

September 8th – The first episode of *Only Fools and Horses* is shown.

1982
November 2nd – Channel 4 is launched with *Countdown* its first programme.

November 5th – The first episode of *The Tube* is broadcast on Channel 4 from the Tyne Tees Television studios in Newcastle.

1983
January 17th – Breakfast Time is broadcast for the first time by the BBC. It is Britain's first early morning television programme.

February 1st – TV-am begins broadcasting with presenters David Frost and Anna Ford.

June 15th – The first episode of *The Black Adder* is shown with Consett-born Rowan Atkinson in the title role. Alnwick Castle is used for location filming.

November 11th – *Auf Wiedersehen, Pet* starts its first series on ITV.

1984
September 23rd – *Threads*, a drama showing the effect of a nuclear war in Britain, is broadcast by the BBC.

1985
February 19th – The first episode of *EastEnders* is shown.

July 13th – The Live Aid concerts are broadcast from Wembley and the John F. Kennedy Stadium in Philadelphia. Amongst the musicians taking part are Sting, Bryan Ferry and Dire Straits.

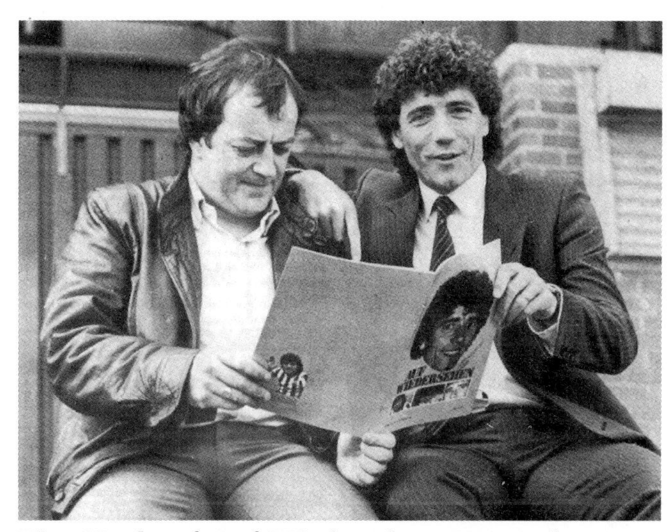

Tim Healy of *Auf Wiedersehen, Pet* reads *Auf Wiedersehen, Kev* – a book celebrating Kevin Keegan's time at Newcastle United

1986
December 25th – Over 30 million viewers watch Den Watts give his wife Angie divorce papers on *EastEnders*.

1987
December 25th – Hilda Ogden makes her final appearance in *Coronation Street*.

1988
November 8th – The wedding of Jason Donovan and Kylie Minogue in *Neighbours* is watched by 20 million viewers when broadcast by the BBC.

1989
February 5th – Sky, Britain's first satellite TV service, begins broadcasting.

November 2nd – The last episode of *Blackadder Goes Forth*, set during the First World War, ends with Rowan Atkinson and Tony Robinson (*seen left on the Radio Times*) going over the top. The screen then fades to a field of poppies.

November 8th – The first episode of *Byker Grove* is shown.

The MetroCentre

The MetroCentre was the idea of North East businessman Sir John Hall (*right*) who developed a former industrial site into the biggest shopping centre in Europe. When it opened in 1986, Sir John welcomed the North East public to 'the shopping revolution':

'On a rainy day in March 1980 I stood near the spot and viewed a piece of land that looked like a flooded moonscape. Six years later that piece of land has been transformed and I am proud to be able to welcome you to a shopping revolution – the most exciting retail scheme ever seen. What brings me greatest personal satisfaction is that Europe's largest out of town shopping centre has been created by the people of the North East, for the people of the North East. The region's firms have built this outstanding complex creating many local new jobs in the process. It is the North East public who will enjoy the benefits of shopping here where the biggest names in the retailing world have gathered under one roof. The MetroCentre will change your life – as it will the very nature of shopping in the North East.'

Left: An aerial view of Dunston Power Station, being built in the 1930s, that generated electricity for the region for over 40 years. Its six chimneys became a landmark by the Tyne and can be glimpsed in the film *Get Carter* during the funeral scene filmed across the river in Newcastle. By the late 1970s the area surrounding the power station was an industrial wasteland that had been used as an ash dump. It was this land that was bought for £100,000 for the future site of the MetroCentre. Most of the power station buildings were demolished and a branch of the American warehouse chain Costco stands here today.

Left: A postcard view of the interior of the MetroCentre. When it first opened in 1986 amongst the high street names at the new shopping centre was the first out of town Marks & Spencer store in the country. Another one of the first shops was Athena who declared they were offering: 'A new concept in bookselling in a bright modern environment.'

Right: An advert for Metroland that opened in February 1988. Located inside the MetroCentre, it was Europe's largest indoor amusement park at that time.

As well as numerous rides, Metroland also had Joker's Green, a nine-hole golf course; Cinema 180 where films were projected on a 180 degree dome; and the Wizard's Castle play park with soft walls, a mirror maze, spiral slides, climbing nets and ball crawls.

The rides were paid for by tokens you bought in advance – rides varied from one to four tokens. In 1988 the prices were:

50 pence for two tokens
£1.40 for six tokens
£2.70 for 12 tokens
All day pass for £3.50

Metroland (*above*) cost £20 million to build and further investments were made over the next decade. In 2006 the MetroCentre announced plans to redevelop the Yellow Mall, meaning the demolition of the amusement park. A campaign was launched to save Metroland but its closure went ahead and the final visitors enjoyed the rides on Sunday, 20th April 2008.

Left: Some youngsters try out the helicopter ride in 1988. In the background is the roller coaster track.

Stop, I Want To Get Off

As a teenager I loved going to Metroland with my friends. We would spend hours there on our favourite rides – the Waltzer, the swinging pirate ship, the flying chairs that spun you around, the little train and the roller coaster. Years later I would take my little niece, Natalie, and my Mam. Even from an early age Natalie showed no fear on any of the rides. My Mam, however, had a real fright on the roller coaster. It went twice around Metroland, stopping briefly after the first circuit then off again for the second one. The first time around was enough for Mam and when the roller coaster came to a halt she screamed at the operator that she needed to get off. He quickly ran to her and off she went. Mam has stayed clear of rides ever since.

Sharyn Taylor

Childhood Toys

Christmas Memories

In the photograph on the right I am at my friend Deborah's home at Christmas in 1985. I had come to visit to show her my new toys and to see what she had received off Santa. I am dressed in a very fashionable 1980s outfit of red satin blouse, black leather tie and black skirt. I was off to my youth club party after visiting Deborah.

My favourite gift that year was a Barbie doll with glittery clothes and a beauty parlour. Deborah also had a Barbie (a fitness model) with a Ken doll. Other presents were Pac-Man, Scrabble and Yahtzee.

There is also the wonderful Barbie McDonald's counter and table which belonged to Deborah. This is now a collectable vintage toy.

Sharyn Taylor

ELECTRONIC GAME
GRANDSTAND
INVADER FROM SPACE
ARCADE-LIKE ACTION

They Came From Outer Space ...

One Christmas in the early 1980s I was very lucky when I received not one but two versions of Space Invaders games. The first was the Grandstand 'Invader from Space' seen on the left. It was one of the earliest electronic hand held games that was produced. The other version of Space Invaders I had was a game on a digital watch. Today, 'wearable tech' is common with watches that have dozens of different functions but back then it was rare. I loved that Space Invader watch but it did get me into trouble at school when I tried to have a sneaky game when I thought the teacher wasn't looking. The best version of Space Invaders that I remember playing was the Atari (*advertised below in the comic 2000AD*). A friend of mine had the console with the games loaded using a cartridge. I used to look forward to the 'Atari nights' at his house.

Andrew Clark

Walkman

Well before iPods and MP3 players, the Sony Walkman was the best way to listen to your music when on the move. The portable cassette player was launched in Japan in 1979 and in Britain the following year. Over the next thirty years, 385 million Walkmans were sold.

Rubik's Cube

The Rubik's Cube – originally called the Magic Cube – was invented by Hungarian Erno Rubik in 1974. By 1980 it was a best selling toy around the world. The aim of the Cube is to twist each face until the six stickers on each side are the same colour. In the age before 'cheats' could be discovered on the internet, many frustrating hours could be spent solving the puzzle that was the Rubik's Cube.

Cabbage Patch Dolls

When she was young, my sister Suzanne was inseparable from her Cabbage Patch doll. In every photograph in the mid 1980s she is always holding her doll tightly. One time when we were going on holiday to Scotland, Suzanne forget her precious Cabbage Patch. She was so upset my Dad drove us all back home, even though we were half way there. Once Suzanne had the doll back in her arms we went on our way back to Scotland.

Sharyn Taylor

My sister Suzanne, holding on to her Cabbage Patch Doll, with me and my brother John in Scotland.

Teddy Ruxpin

Another best selling toy was Teddy Ruxpin – the talking bear manufactured by World of Wonder. When Teddy Ruxpin was launched in 1985 it was the world's first animated talking toy. Its mouth and eyes would move while an audio tape in the toy's back read a story.

The most popular toys of the 1980s

1980 – Rubik's Cube – £1

1981 – LEGO train set – £32

1982 – BMX Bike – £45

The BMX Bi-Weekly magazine.

1983 – Cabbage Patch Kids – £15

1984 – Transformers – £10

1985 – Care Bears – £15

1986 – Lazer tag – £50

1987 – Koosh Ball – £2

A Koosh Ball is made of rubber strings attached to a soft core.

1988 – Ghostbusters toys – £10

1989 – Game Boy – £50

Sporting Times

Glen McCrory (*left*) became the North East's first World Boxing Champion when he defeated Patrick Lumumba for the IBF Cruiserweight belt at the Louisa Centre in Stanley in 1989. He started his career at twelve years old when he joined Consett Amateur Boxing Club and made his professional debut in 1984. Three years later he won the Commonwealth Cruiserweight title in Gateshead. The Annfield Plain boxer made one successful defence of his World title before losing to American Jeff Lampkin in 1990. Following this defeat McCrory moved up to heavyweight and in September 1991 was beaten by Lennox Lewis in a bout for the British and European titles (*right*). 'Gentleman' Glen retired in 1993 and later wrote his autobiography *Carrying David* – its title inspired by his adopted brother David who suffered from a muscle wasting disease.

Right: Steve Cram taking part in the Chester-le-Street Fun Run in 1983. The Jarrow athlete was part of the golden generation of British middle distance runners of the 1980s that included Steve Ovett and Sebastian Coe.

Cram won the gold medal for 1500 metres at the World Championships in 1983 and at the Commonwealth Games and European Championships in 1982 and 1986. The only title that eluded him was the Olympics. The closest he came was in Los Angeles in 1984 when he claimed the 1500 metres silver medal; finishing second to Seb Coe. The following year Cram broke three world records in 19 days – 1500 metres, the mile and 2000 metres. Towards the end of his career, he suffered a number of injuries and retired in 1994, becoming a television presenter.

'The atmosphere is so tense, if Elvis walked in with a portion of chips, you could hear the vinegar sizzle on them' – a classic quote from Sid Waddell (*left*). In the 1980s Sid Waddell did much to popularise darts on television with his unique presenting style. He spent his early years in Lynemouth in Northumberland before going on to Cambridge University. A career in the media followed and as well as commentating on his beloved darts, he wrote biographies, novels and television programmes such as *Jossy's Giants* – the story of a Geordie football manager *(left)*. Sadly Sid died in 2012. The following year the World Darts Championship trophy was named in his honour.

North East Football Time Line

1980

May 12th – Sunderland beat West Ham United 2-0 to clinch promotion to the First Division.

1981

April 25th – Whickham win the FA Vase at Wembley. Five thousand Whickham fans travelled to London to see their team beat Willenhall Town 3-2.

July/August 1981 – Middlesbrough sell David Armstrong, Craig Johnston and Mark Proctor for a total of almost £2 million. The club is relegated from the First Division at the end of the 1981-82 season.

October 1st – Chester-le-Street-born Bryan Robson becomes Britain's most expensive footballer in a £1.5 million move from West Bromwich Albion to Manchester United.

The Whickham players and staff celebrate winning the FA Vase in 1981. They were the last North East team to win a final at the old Wembley Stadium.

Bryan Robson played for Manchester United until 1994. The former England captain then became player-manager at Middlesbrough.

In the summer of 1981 Sunderland unveiled a radical new strip – seen on the right in a friendly against Newcastle at Roker Park. Gone were the traditional red and white stripes to be replaced by thin, double red stripes on a white shirt. Red shorts replaced the black that had been worn since 1973. After two years Sunderland reverted back to a broader striped shirt.

1982

July 5th – England draw 0–0 with hosts Spain and are eliminated from the World Cup. Ron Greenwood retires as England manager and is succeeded by Sacriston-born Bobby Robson two days later. Robson was manager of the successful Ipswich team who won the FA Cup in 1978 and UEFA Cup in 1981.

August 28th – Kevin Keegan makes his debut for Newcastle United against QPR. Keegan scores the only goal in a 1-0 victory.

Bobby Robson at a press conference while England manager in the 1980s.

Jack Charlton enjoying one of his favourite pastimes, fishing. Jack was only in charge at Newcastle for one season then later found success as the manager of the Republic of Ireland.

1984

May 12th – Kevin Keegan plays his last competitive match for Newcastle in a 3-1 win for over Brighton. The Magpies are promoted to the First Division.

August 14 – Jack Charlton becomes Newcastle manager.

1985

March 24th – Sunderland face Norwich City in the Milk Cup Final at Wembley. Norwich win 1-0 with an own goal scored by Gordon Chisholm. Sunderland's Clive Walker misses a penalty. The Black Cats are relegated from the First Division at the end of the season.

April 13th – Paul Gascoigne makes his first team debut for Newcastle as a substitute against Queen's Park Rangers at St James' Park.

July 1st – Chris Waddle leaves Newcastle to join Tottenham Hotspur for a fee of £590,000.

The programme for the Milk Cup Final – Sunderland v Norwich City in 1985.

Left: Chris Waddle in action for Newcastle United.

1986

May – Darlington finish 13th in the Third Division – their highest placing since four divisions were introduced in 1958.

June 22nd – England are out of the World Cup after being beaten 2-1 by Argentina. Diego Maradona scores one goal with his hand (nicknamed the 'Hand of God') and then dribbles past half the England team to score the second. Playing that day were North East-born players Terry Fenwick, Peter Beardsley, Chris Waddle and Trevor Steven as well as future Sunderland managers – Terry Butcher and Peter Reid.

August 23rd – Middlesbrough play their first game of the season at Hartlepool's Victoria Ground. The Teesside club were on the verge of liquidation and were unable to play at their home ground of Ayresome Park whose gates were padlocked. The game against Port Vale was played at Hartlepool as Middlesbrough were being threatened with being kicked out of the Football League if they did not fulfil their first fixture of the season. Chairman Steve Gibson put together a last minute consortium, that included ICI and Scottish & Newcastle Breweries, to save the club.

Middlesbrough's Bernie Slaven who played in the match at Hartlepool's ground in 1986.

Marco Gabbiadini who was signed by Sunderland from York City in August 1987.

1987

May 14th & 17th – In a two-legged play off, Sunderland are beaten by Gillingham and are relegated to the Third Division.

July 14th – Liverpool pay a record fee between two English clubs with the £1.9 million transfer of Peter Beardsley from Newcastle.

1988

April 30th – Sunderland beat Port Vale 1-0 and are promoted back into the Second Division. The top scorer that season was Marco Gabbiadini.

July 18th – Paul Gascoigne leaves Newcastle United for Tottenham Hotspur for £2.2 million.

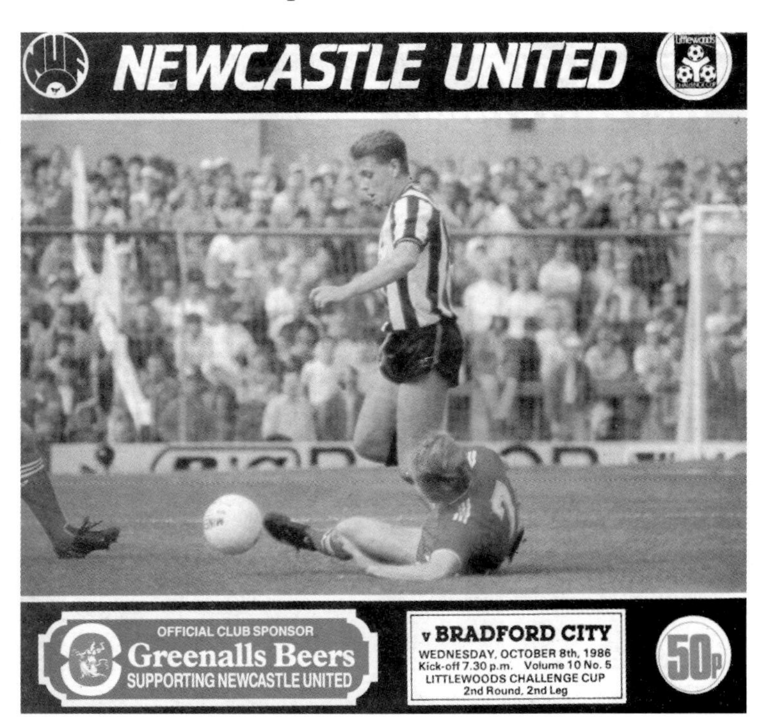

Right: Paul Gascoigne on the cover of a Newcastle programme in 1986. After making his debut in 1985, the young midfielder quickly became one of the exciting prospects in the country. In 1988 he was voted Young Player of the Year by the Professional Footballers Association. Two years later he helped England reach the semi-final of the World Cup in Italy.

A Fashionable Decade

In the photograph on the right I am with my sister Suzanne and brother John meeting Santa at Binns in 1982. All three of us are wearing our new checked tweed coats. At this time in the early '80s tweed coats were very fashionable.

As I got older and became a teenager I was very interested in the latest fashions. Some of the trends I remember wearing at that time include: puff ball skirt, jumper dress, satin blouse, fake fur coat, plastic bracelets and beads. Every Saturday I would go with my friends to Tammy Girl that was part of the Etam chain of shops. We would spend hours looking at all the clothes and the new styles. Another popular 1980s shop was Geordie Jeans where I bought my denim jacket and stone washed jeans.

Reading magazines such as *Jackie* also gave us tips on the best outfits to wear. One of my favourite 'looks' was a black turtle neck jumper and beige chinos with a thin brown belt. On my feet were Pods or Kicker shoes. To complete the outfit we would have our hair curly permed.

Sharyn Taylor

My very fashionable sister Suzanne wearing a black turtle neck and chinos with a curly perm in the late 1980s.

Geordie Jeans was founded in 1978 and had their factory in South Shields. The jeans, the cheapest around in the 1980s, were very popular and at one time the firm had ten shops in the region. Their distinctive logo was the flat cap wearing Geordie seen on the right. By the late 1990s, increased costs and competition led to the closure of the factory and then the shops. However,

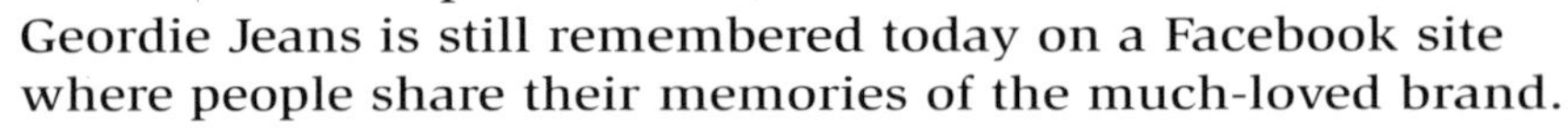

Geordie Jeans is still remembered today on a Facebook site where people share their memories of the much-loved brand.

Left: The cover of the magazine *Jackie* from 17th April 1982. Inside were features on fashion, beauty, pop, photo stories, tips for passing exams and a Duran Duran pin up. *Jackie* was launched in 1964 by the publisher D.C. Thomson of Dundee. The children's author Jacqueline Wilson worked on the early editions. Declining sales saw the magazine close in 1993.

Some other female styles from the decade included: jump suits, shoulder pads, leg warmers, headbands, lace gloves and jelly shoes. Also popular for a time were neon coloured clothes and polka dots.

Female fashion icons of the 1980s were Madonna, Jane Fonda, Jerry Hall and Joan Collins in Dynasty.

Men's Fashion – Highs & Lows

As a teenager in the 1980s I remember a number of men's fashions through the decade. In the early '80s I went with a group of friends to a concert at Newcastle City Hall when the 'New Romantic' style was all the rage. Two of my mates were wearing black bibbed cavalry shirts and jodhpurs!

In the mid 1980s the TV show *Miami Vice* was a big influence and men wore white or pastel coloured suits (with sleeves rolled up) with a t-shirt or vest. Another style at that time was 'casual' which was normally a patterned jumper, grey trousers, white socks and slip on shoes.

By 1987 I was into my student days with black jeans, cardigan, Doc Martins and a 'big' coat. I was very comfortable with this style and I haven't changed much thirty years later.

Andrew Clark

Don Johnson in a typical outfit from TV's *Miami Vice*.

Left: Eight teenage lads sporting the casual look in 1984. They are at Roker Park to sign schoolboy forms for Sunderland and are with the club's Youth Development Officer, George Herd, who is wearing his pin-striped suit and kipper tie. Next to him is Gary Owers who went on to play for Sunderland in the 1992 FA Cup Final.

A very popular men's hair style in the 1980s and early '90s was the notorious 'Mullet'. Two North East footballers, Chris Waddle (*right*) and Barry Venison (*far right*) were well known for their hair that was long at the back while short at the front and sides.

The term mullet is thought to have been first used by the American rap group the Beastie Boys. In an interview they made fun of the haircut and said they called it a mullet. 'Mullet Head' is an old American phrase to describe someone who is stupid. It is used by the author Mark Twain in his book *Adventures of Huckleberry Finn* and by the actor George Kennedy in the film *Cool Hand Luke*.

Chris Waddle did not have a mullet for the whole of the 1980s and for a time had a much shorter haircut. That style is seen on the right on the cover of *Diamond Lights,* the single he recorded with Tottenham team-mate Glenn Hoddle. *Diamond Lights* reached number 12 in the charts and Glenn & Chris appeared on *Top of the Pops*.

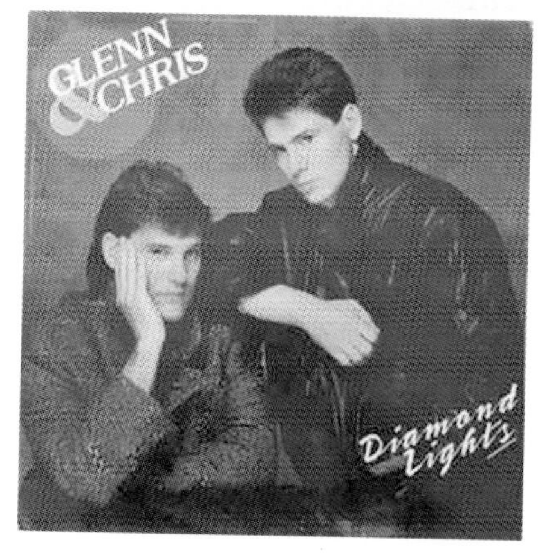

Movie Memories

Right: The staff of the Wallaw in Ashington on the day it closed on 2nd August 1982. This was the last of five cinemas that were once in the town. Many local cinemas closed during the 1980s with the end of the decade seeing the opening of the multiplexes.

The Roar of the Crowd

I enjoying going to today's multiplexes with all of their modern facilities, however, I do miss the old fashioned cinemas I remember from my teenage years. In the 1980s I would go with friends to the late night horror double bills at the ABC in Sunderland to see films such as *Creepshow* and *Return of the Dawn of the Dead*. I think some of the audience had come straight from the pub and it was often a very rowdy night watching the films. One time the police were called by the staff to restore calm.

Another film I remember was the action-packed *Aliens* – the sequel to *Alien*. Again it was a very noisy audience and more like a football match then a night at the pictures. At the end of the film, when Sigourney Weaver takes on the final alien, there were great roars of encouragement from the audience and I am sure there were people standing on the seats at the back. With the backing of the roar of the crowd, Sigourney blasted the alien into outer space with a round of applause and more cheering.

Andrew Clark

Warner opened their multiplex cinema at Manors in Newcastle (*right*) on 6th December 1989. With over three thousand seats and nine screens with 70mm projection and Dolby Stereo sound, the latest film technology had come to the North East. The cinema held a free open day with screenings of the 1980s classics: *Indiana Jones and the Last Crusade, Rain Man, Twins, Mississippi Burning, Licence to Kill, Dangerous Liaisons, Naked Gun* and *Working Girl* as well as Loony Tunes Cartoons. The audience were given complimentary Pepsi and popcorn and there was also the opportunity to meet Phillip Schofield, Caron Keating and the cast of Byker Grove.

The following day there was the premiere of *The Delinquents,* the film debut of the Australian singer and actress Kylie Minogue who was a special guest at the screening.

An advert for the films shown during the first week at the Warner Cinema in 1989. The cinema closed in 2004.

Right: The poster for *Blade Runner* directed by South Shields-born Ridley Scott. The 1982 science fiction epic starring Harrison Ford was one of the most stylish films of the decade. Ridley Scott lived for a time on Teesside and he has acknowledged that the area's industrial landscape influenced the look of the film:

'There's a walk from Redcar into Hartlepool. I would cross a bridge at night and walk above the steel works. So that's probably where the opening of *Blade Runner* comes from. It always seemed to be rather gloomy and raining and I'd just think God, this is beautiful. You can find beauty in everything and so I think I found the beauty in that darkness.'

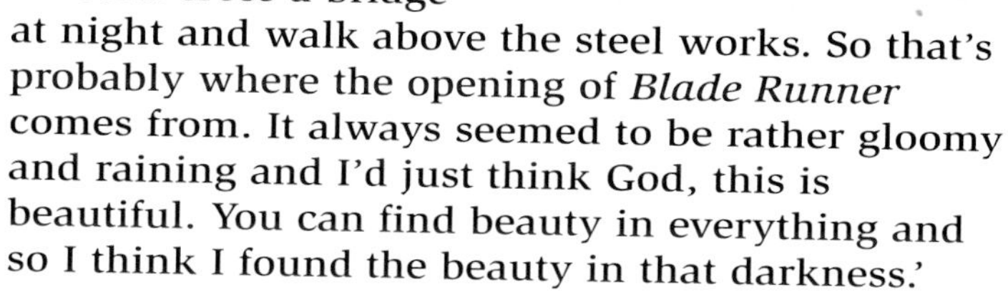

Ridley Scott (*above*) directed his first feature film, *The Duellists*, in 1977 and his other films include *Alien*, *Thelma & Louise*, *Black Hawk Down* and the Oscar-winning *Gladiator*. He was knighted in 2003.

Before his film debut, Scott was one of the best directors of commercials in the country. His most famous advert from the 1970s was for Hovis where a young lad struggles up a cobblestone hill on his delivery bike. In 1984 he directed another memorable commercial at a cost of $1.5 million for the launch of Apple's Macintosh computer (*right*). It was shown during the Super Bowl and was inspired by George Orwell's novel *1984*.

The most popular films of the 1980s

1980 – The Empire Strikes Back

1981 – Raiders of the Lost Ark

1982 – E.T. The Extra-Terrestrial

1983 – Return of the Jedi

1984 – Beverly Hills Cop

1985 – Back to the Future

1986 – Top Gun

The blockbuster *Top Gun* was directed by Tony Scott who was born in Tynemouth. His first involvement in the film industry was when he acted in a short film directed by his brother Ridley. Tony followed his older brother into directing commercials and then on to Hollywood. His other films in the 1980s included *The Hunger* starring David Bowie and *Beverly Hills Cop II* with Eddie Murphy.

1987 – Three Men and a Baby

1988 – Rain Man

1989 – Indiana Jones and the Last Crusade

Right: Film director Franc Roddam working with Sting and Jennifer Beals on the set of the 1985 film *The Bride* which was based on the novel *Frankenstein*. Sting and North East-born Roddam had previously worked together on *Quadrophenia*.

Left: The poster for the film *Stormy Monday* that was filmed in the North East and released in 1988. It was directed by Mike Figgis who had spent his early years in Newcastle. One of the stars was Sting who is featured in the poster on the High Level Bridge with Hollywood actor Tommy Lee Jones. Sting plays a nightclub owner who is being threatened by corrupt developers who want to take over his club on Newcastle's Quayside. A television series, *Finney*, was later produced which was based on the character played by Sting. In the TV programme the title role was taken by David Morrissey.

In the 1980s Sting also appeared in the films *Brimstone and Treacle*, *Dune* and *The Adventures of Baron Munchausen*.

Mike Figgis went on to have a successful career, directing films such as *Internal Affairs*, *The Browning Version* and *Leaving Las Vegas*.

The First Video Recorders

Today if you miss your favourite television shows you can easily see them with catch up TV or dvd box sets. In the early 1980s if I wasn't at home to watch *Doctor Who* or *The Incredible Hulk* then I would probably never get the chance see the show again. That changed when we got our first video recorder. I remember the excitement when my parents bought our first machine with its clunky cassettes used to tape the programmes. I guess there was a similar excitement in the 1950s when televisions started to appear in people's homes.

We also rented films from the many local video shops that were around then. You normally paid a membership fee of around £10 then renting a film for a night was about £2, or £4 for a few days. There are only a handful of such shops left in the whole of the country.

Most of the films on offer were ones from the 1970s and it seemed to take ages for the new releases to be available. Now films are on sale as dvds or on satellite and streaming shortly after they have been shown in the cinema.

Andrew Clark

An advert from the mid 1980s for Benton Hypermarket who had a VHS video recorder available for £369.

Days to Remember

After the closure of Sacriston Colliery in County Durham in 1985 it was not only miners who lost their jobs. Also looking for new work was 'Pip' the pit pony who moved to the nearby Beamish Open Air Museum. On the left he is being introduced to Princess Anne when she visited Beamish to open the Carriage House at the museum in 2002. Horsepower continued to be used in British coalmines until 1994 with 'Flax' being the last pit pony in the country when its work came to an end at Ellington Colliery.

In 1980 Newcastle celebrated the 900th anniversary of the building of the castle in 1080 by Robert Curthose, the son of William the Conqueror. This was a timber structure that was replaced a century later by a stone castle – the Castle Keep that stands today dates from this time. The celebrations in 1980 included a water pageant on the Tyne with Viking longships, a visit from Wimbledon champion Bjorn Borg and a replica of Stephenson's Rocket on display at the Civic Centre. There were also exhibitions housed in 'poly air domes' situated by the University (*above an artist's impression*).

The supersonic airliner Concorde made its first visit to the region in August 1983. Thousands of people went to see it at Newcastle Airport and 100 passengers were on board for a demonstration flight over the North Sea.

Right: A poster for the musical *Katie Mulholland* performed at Newcastle Playhouse in 1983. Catherine Cookson's novel was adapted for the stage by Ken Hill with music and lyrics by Sunderland-born Eric Boswell. Six years later the first of the popular TV films based on Catherine Cookson's work was produced by Tyne Tees Television. *Fifteen Streets* starred Sean Bean and Owen Teale and its success led to a further seventeen films based on the books of the best-selling Tyneside author.

The floating nightclub the *Tuxedo Princess* was opened in December 1983. The idea to turn a former car ferry into one of Tyneside's premier attractions came from local businessman Michael Quadrini who also owned the Newcastle nightclub Tuxedo Junction. It was moored under the Tyne Bridge on the Gateshead side and soon became known simply as 'The Boat'.

When it opened, the *Tuxedo Princess* was advertised as: 'Newcastle's most talked about ship since the Mauretania is about to throw down its gangplanks to welcome the city's sophisticated Christmas revellers.'

The original name of the ship was the *Caledonian Princess* and it was a roll on/roll off car ferry built in 1961 that served the cross Channel and Irish Sea routes. It was four hundred feet long with five decks and as a ferry carried up to 1,300 passengers. After conversion to a nightclub, the main deck became Di Angelo's Pizzeria while another deck was Diane's Discotheque. There was also the Cunard Cocktail Bar.

The *Tuxedo Princess* remained a popular destination for revellers for the next decade before it was moved to Glasgow. The nightclub *Tuxedo Royale* then took its place on the Tyne. When the *Princess* returned to Gateshead, the *Royale* was moved to the Tees in 2000. The final night on the Tyne for the *Tuxedo Princess* was in December 2007 and the ship left the river the following year. Its final destination was a breakers yard in Greece.

An advert from December 1983 introducing the *Tuxedo Princess* – 'Europe's Premier Floating Palace of Leisure.'

Right: The poster for The Police in concert at Gateshead International Stadium on 31st July 1982. One of the support bands that day was the Irish band U2 who were later to become one of the biggest rock acts in the world. The previous year the athletics stadium had hosted the 'Rock on the Tyne Festival' over the August Bank Holiday weekend. Hundreds of fans travelled from all round the country to camp on grassland next to the venue. Ian Dury, Elvis Costello, Dr Feelgood, Lindisfarne and U2 were some of those who entertained the crowd of 15,000.

In the 1980s the biggest names in the music world came to Newcastle United's St James' Park to perform before the largest audiences ever seen up to that time for concerts in the North East. The first band to appear at St James' was the Rolling Stones in 1982 with a ticket price of £8.50. A crowd of 38,000 meant a pay day for Newcastle United of around £35,000 for hosting the event at their ground. The Rolling Stones were followed by Bob Dylan in 1984 (tickets £11) and Bruce Springsteen the following year (tickets £14).

In 1986 it was the turn of Queen to rock St James' Park with supporting acts Status Quo and INXS (*advertised below*). Queen had just released their single *A Kind of Magic* used in the film *Highlander* and their *Greatest Hits* LP was one of the biggest selling albums of the decade. Tickets for the gig cost £13 and were available by post, credit card hot line and venues round the North East. When the tickets first went on sale three months before the concert they were sold out in two and half hours. Sales for Queen were much quicker than for the Rolling Stones, Bob Dylan and Bruce Springsteen.

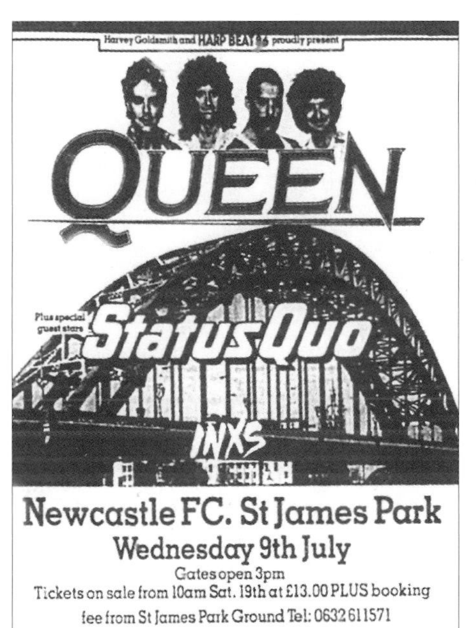

Rebuilding work at St James' Park in 1987 meant the next big concert in the region was in Sunderland. The switch to Roker Park may have confused the star of the show, David Bowie (*left*), who welcomed the 36,000 fans with a cry of 'Good evening Newcastle.'

Red Wedge

The best concert I ever went to was 'Red Wedge' at Newcastle City Hall in January 1986. The Red Wedge tour was organised by Billy Bragg, Paul Weller and other musicians to highlight political issues through music. I remember that we were given a 'goody bag' filled with information about the Labour Party, Greenpeace, Save the Whales and the Campaign for Nuclear Disarmament.

As well as Bragg and Weller (*right*), other musicians that night included Tom Robinson, The Communards, Prefab Sprout, The Kane Gang and Alan Hull of Lindisfarne. The highlight of the night was when it was announced that special guests The Smiths were to appear. The Manchester band were at their peak at the time and their four-song set was brilliant.

Andrew Clark

Left: An advert for leisure activities that were available at Kielder Water shortly after it opened. Work on the reservoir began in the mid 1970s and the site was officially opened by the Queen in 1982. Kielder quickly became a popular visitor attraction. This advert from the 1980s gives a description of the area:

'Enjoy the absolute freedom of Kielder Water, Europe's largest man-made lake set in the wild and beautiful Northumbrian countryside!

'There's so much to see and do – dinghy and board sailing, sail or motor cruising, canoeing, angling, sub-aqua, riding, back-packing, walking, picnicking or painting and photographing the breathtaking splendour of this vast, unspoilt water wonderland.'

Our First Holiday Abroad

In 1980 my parents booked a family holiday with Sun Seeker of Middlesbrough (*advertised right*). We travelled from the North East to Lloret de Mar on the Costa Brava by road on a coach – a distance of over a thousand miles! The coach first went to Dover and we crossed the channel by Hovercraft before going on to Paris for a one night stop-over. When we arrived in Spain we spent two weeks sleeping in one of the large tents featured in the advert. Then it was back on the coach for another thousand miles to get home.

Andrew Clark

Left: Dad, Mam, me and sister Paula on a stop-over in Paris on our way to the Costa Brava in 1980. Package holidays to France and Spain were becoming more common in the early '80s.

In September 1988 plans were unveiled to redevelop the East Quayside area of Newcastle (*right*). Old warehouses and other commercial buildings were to be demolished to make way for hotels, bars, restaurants and leisure facilities on the banks of the Tyne. One of the few buildings that would remain was the former CWS Warehouse that was to be converted into a hotel. Other developments included prestigious offices and apartments. A public exhibition was opened by the Quayside to showcase the plans.

An aerial view of Newcastle and Gateshead from around 1990. In the following decade the area on the banks of the Tyne would be transformed. The first development on the Quayside was the new Law Courts (1), opened in 1990. The derelict CWS Warehouse (2) was brought back to life as the Malmaison Hotel in 1997. On the opposite bank (3), The Sage concert venue was built and opened in 2004. Those three buildings in 2018 are shown below. By the turn of the 21st century, the Baltic Centre for Contemporary Art and the Millennium Bridge were added to the regeneration of the Quayside.

Law Courts.

The Malmaison Hotel.

The Sage.

1980s Time Line

1980

January 29th – The Rubik's Cube makes its international debut at the British Toy and Hobby Fair in London.

February 2nd – Britain's Robin Cousins wins the gold medal in the men's figure skating at the Winter Olympic Games in Lake Placid, New York.

April 30th – Terrorists take over the Iranian embassy in London. The SAS retakes the Embassy on May 5th.

June 30th – The pre-decimal sixpence coin is withdrawn from circulation.

August 11th – The Tyne and Wear Metro opens with the first service being between the Haymarket and Tynemouth.

September 9th – The Liverpool-registered oil carrier MV *Derbyshire* sinks with the loss of all 44 crew off Japan in a typhoon. The ship was built at Swan Hunter's in Wallsend.

September 12th – Consett Steelworks closes with the loss of 4,500 jobs. The town now has the highest rate of unemployment in the UK.

November 4th – Republican challenger Ronald Reagan defeats incumbent Democratic President Jimmy Carter to become the 40th President of the United States.

December 8th – John Lennon is shot dead in New York City by Mark Chapman.

1981

January 20th – Iran releases 52 American hostages held for 444 days.

March 29th – The first London Marathon starts with 7,500 runners.

April 4th – UK pop group Bucks Fizz's song *Making Your Mind Up* wins the Eurovision Song Contest in Dublin.

May 5th – Bobby Sands, a member of the Provisional IRA, dies on hunger strike while in the Maze Prison.

May 22nd – Peter Sutcliffe, the Yorkshire Ripper, is found guilty of 13 counts of murder and seven of attempted murder. He is sentenced to life imprisonment. During the investigation hoax letters and a tape were sent to the police from Wearside.

June 20th – HMS *Ark Royal* is launched from Swan Hunter's shipyard.

June 28th – The first Great North Run is held – 12,264 start the race with 10,665 finishing.

July 29th – The Prince of Wales and Lady Diana Spencer are married at St Paul's Cathedral in London.

October 26th – The band Queen release their *Greatest Hits* album. It goes on to sell over six million copies in the UK and 25 million around the world.

Princess Diana made several visits to the North East. Here she shakes hands with families in Sunderland in 1990.

1982

January 26th – Unemployment increases by 129,918 to 3,070,621 – 11.5% of the workforce was unemployed at that time.

April 2nd – Argentina invades and occupies the Falkland Islands. Britain sends a naval taskforce to retake the islands.

May 2nd – The nuclear submarine HMS *Conqueror* sinks the Argentine cruiser *General Belgrano*, killing 323 sailors.

May 4th – HMS *Sheffield* is hit by an Exocet missile with 20 sailors killed.

May 26th – The official opening of Kielder Water, the largest artificial lake in the UK by capacity. It is surrounded by Kielder Forest, the largest planted woodland in Europe.

June 9th – The twenty pence coin first goes into circulation.

June 11th – The film *E.T. The Extra-Terrestrial* is released in the United States. Directed by Steven Spielberg, it become the biggest box-office hit of the decade.

June 14th – Argentine forces in Stanley, the capital of the Falklands Islands, surrender.

June 21 – Prince William is born at St Mary's Hospital, London.

1983

January 31st – Seatbelts for drivers and front seat passengers becomes mandatory in the UK.

May 16th – Wheel clamps are first used to combat illegal parking in London.

June 9th – The Conservative Government, led by Margaret Thatcher, wins the General Election by a landslide majority. Among the new members of parliament are three Labour MPs – Tony Blair (for Sedgefield), Gordon Brown and Jeremy Corbyn.

July 16th – The centenary Durham Miners' Gala is held.

October 2nd – Neil Kinnock is elected leader of the Labour Party, replacing Michael Foot.

November 18th – Janet Walton from Liverpool gives birth to female sextuplets.

Right: Miners and their families parade with a banner through the streets of Durham during the centenary gala in 1983. The first Miners' Gala, or Big Meeting as it is called, was held at Wharton Park, Durham in 1871 and in its heyday up to 300,000 people would attend. The gala was cancelled during both world wars and during strikes in the 1920s, so the centenary was held in 1983. The following year saw the beginning of the miners' strike.

1984

February 14th – Jayne Torvill and Christopher Dean win the gold medal for ice dancing at the Winter Olympic Games in Sarajevo, Yugoslavia.

March 6th – The National Coal Board announces that 20 collieries are to be closed. The miners go on a strike that lasts almost a year.

June 20th – The Government announces that O-level and CSE exams are to be replaced by a new exam – the GCSE.

September 15th – The Princess of Wales gives birth to her second son, Prince Harry.

October 12th – During the Conservative Party Conference in Brighton, the Provisional IRA explode a bomb at the Grand Hotel. Anthony Berry MP and four other people are killed. Norman Tebbit is rescued from the rubble while Margaret Thatcher escapes unharmed.

October 23rd – Michael Buerk reports for BBC News on the famine in Ethiopia.

November 25th – Bob Geldof forms Band Aid to record the charity single *Do They Know It's Christmas?* to raise money for famine relief in Ethiopia. The single is released on December 3rd and becomes the Christmas number one.

1985

January 1st – The first mobile phone calls are made in the UK.

March 3rd – The miners' strike ends. At its peak over 140,000 miners were on strike.

May 11th – A fire in a wooden stand at the Valley Parade football stadium in Bradford kills 56 supporters.

May 29th – Thirty-nine people are killed when a wall collapses at the Heysel Stadium in Brussels after Liverpool supporters charged Juventus fans. UEFA bans all English football clubs from European competitions. The ban lasts for five season for all clubs except Liverpool who are excluded for six years.

July 13th – Live Aid concerts in London and Philadelphia raise over £50 million for famine relief in Ethiopia.

October 6th – Sunderland-born PC Keith Blakelock is fatally stabbed during the Broadwater Farm Riot in Tottenham.

1986

February 9th – Halley's Comet reaches its closest point to the Sun, during its first visit to our solar system since 1910.

April 22nd – The first Bluebird car is built at Nissan's factory in Sunderland. The vehicle was for tests and not for sale.

April 26th – A disaster at the Chernobyl Nuclear Power Plant in the Ukraine sees over 350,000 people relocated away from the area. It is believed thousands of people have died as the result of radiation poisoning.

April 28th – The first phase of the MetroCentre, Europe's largest indoor shopping centre, is opened.

July 2nd – Ian Rush becomes the most expensive British footballer up to that time in a £3.2 million transfer from Liverpool to Juventus.

November – The first UNESCO World Heritage Sites in the UK are announced. One of those chosen is Durham Castle and Cathedral. Other sites include: Stonehenge, the Giants Causeway, and Ironbridge Gorge.

Left: Durham Castle and Cathedral – a UNESCO World Heritage site since 1986.

1987

March 6th – The cross-channel ferry MS *Herald of Free Enterprise* capsizes off Zeebrugge harbour in Belgium – 193 people are killed.

June 11 – The Conservatives, led by Margaret Thatcher, are re-elected for a third term at the General Election.

October 1st – Swedish retailer IKEA opens its first British store at Warrington in Cheshire.

October 15th-16th – Hurricane force winds batter much of south east England, killing 23 people and causing extensive damage to property. BBC weather man Michael Fish said at the time: 'Earlier on today, apparently, a woman rang the BBC and said she heard there was a hurricane on the way; well, if you're watching, don't worry, there isn't.'

December 15th – Construction work begins on the Channel Tunnel.

1988

February 5th – The first Red Nose Day. The Comic Relief appeal raises £15 million for charity.

March 11th – The £1 note ceases to be legal tender.

July 6th – The Piper Alpha production platform in the North Sea is destroyed by explosions and fires, killing 165 oil workers and two rescue workers.

August 22nd – New licensing laws allow pubs to stay open all day in England and Wales.

December 7th – The last shipbuilding yards in Sunderland, once the biggest shipbuilding town in the world, close with the loss of 2,400 jobs.

December 21st – Pan Am Flight 103 explodes over the town of Lockerbie, killing a total of 270 people – 11 on the ground and all 259 on board. In 2001 a Libyan intelligence officer is found guilty of murder in connection with the bombing of the plane.

1989

April 15th – 96 Liverpool fans are killed in a crush of supporters at Hillsborough in Sheffield during their FA Cup semi-final against Nottingham Forest.

April 17th – Home Secretary Douglas Hurd in a statement in Parliament following the Hillsborough Disaster announces that it is the Government's belief that major football grounds should become all-seater. Lord Justice Taylor of Gosforth is appointed to lead a public inquiry into the disaster.

May 26th – Arsenal are First Division Champions after beating Liverpool at Anfield with a goal by Michael Thomas in the final minute of the last game of the season.

August 20th – The pleasure cruiser *Marchioness* collides with a barge in the Thames, killing 51 people.

December 24th – A new version of *Do They Know It's Christmas?* by Band Aid II is the Christmas number one

Right: Football fans on the terraces of Roker Park in the mid 1980s. In the following decade standing at football matches was phased out for the top clubs in Britain.

Also available from Summerhill Books

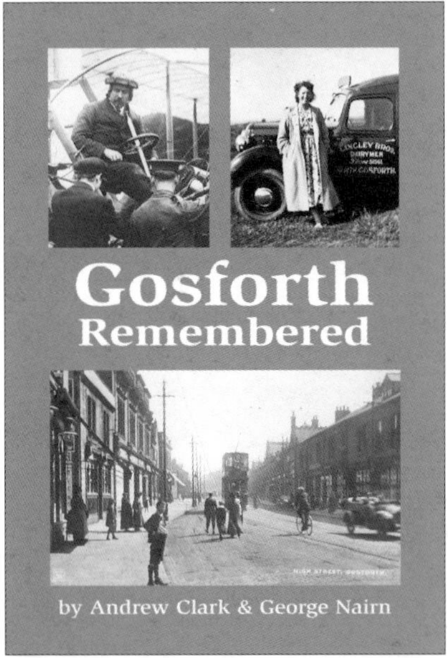

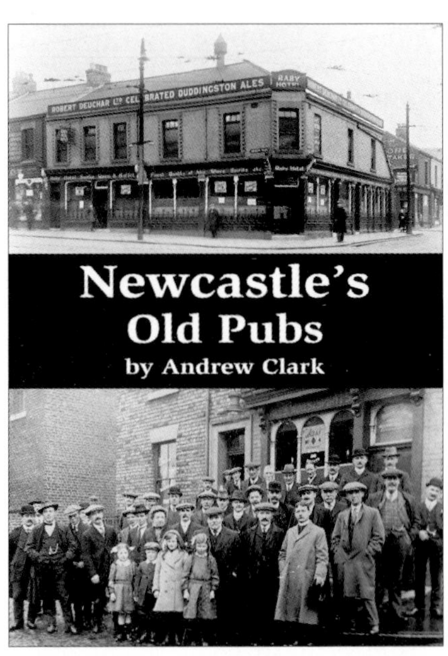

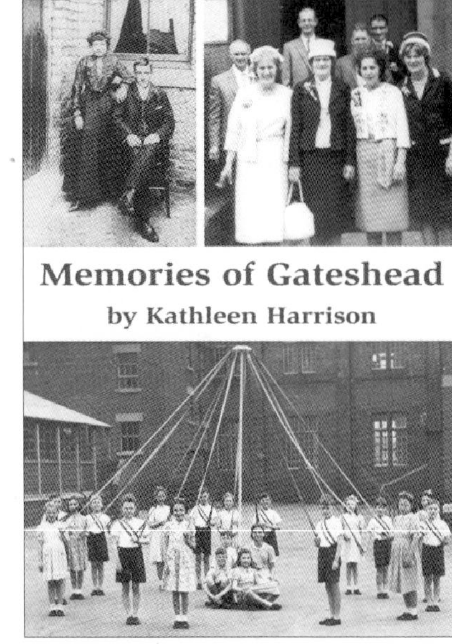

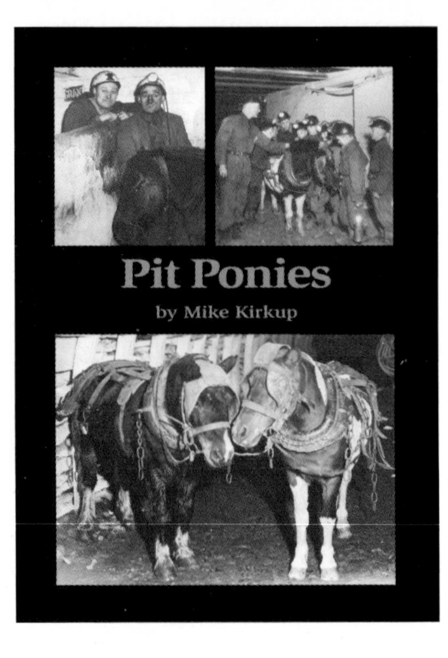

visit our website to view our full range of books
www.summerhillbooks.co.uk